PITTSBURGH PENGUINS

BY WILLIAM ARTHUR

Book design by Maggie Villaume
Cover design by Maggie Villaume

Photographs ©: Gene J. Puskar/AP Images, cover, 10–11; Keith Srakocic/AP Images, 4–5, 21, 23; Carlos Osorio/AP Images, 7; Paul Sancya/AP Images, 9; Horace Cort/AP Images, 13; Paul Benoit/AP Images, 15; Gary Tramontina/AP Images, 16–17; John Swart/AP Images, 19; Mel Evans/AP Images, 24–25; Frank Gunn/The Canadian Press/AP Images, 27; Eric Canha/Cal Sport Media/AP Images, 29

Press Box Books, an imprint of Press Room Editions.

ISBN
978-1-63494-496-0 (library bound)
978-1-63494-522-6 (paperback)
978-1-63494-573-8 (epub)
978-1-63494-548-6 (hosted ebook)

Library of Congress Control Number: 2022902477

Distributed by North Star Editions, Inc.
2297 Waters Drive
Mendota Heights, MN 55120
www.northstareditions.com

Printed in the United States of America
082022

ABOUT THE AUTHOR

William Arthur is a lifelong hockey fan who grew up playing the sport on a frozen pond in Thunder Bay, Ontario. He lives in northwest Ontario with his trusted foxhound.

TABLE OF CONTENTS

1

Sidney Crosby
hangs his head in
defeat at the 2008
Stanley Cup Final.

RESPECT EARNED

Sidney Crosby skated off the ice, defeated. At 20 years old, the skilled center was already a National Hockey League (NHL) superstar. He was not yet a champion, though. His Pittsburgh Penguins had reached the 2008 Stanley Cup Final. However, the Detroit Red Wings turned them away in six games. Crosby and the Penguins still had work to do.

Pittsburgh's 2008–09 season got off to a slow start. But by the playoffs, the Penguins were in top form. And once again, they met the Red Wings in the Final.

The series started poorly for the Penguins. Detroit won the first two games. The Red Wings knew Crosby was a major scoring threat. So, they sent center Henrik Zetterberg and defenseman Nicklas Lidström to slow him down. Crosby was up to the challenge. If he couldn't score, he was going to outwork everyone.

Pittsburgh battled back to tie the series at two games each. The Red Wings

Marc-André Fleury makes a save in Game 7 of the 2009 Stanley Cup Final.

won Game 5, but the Penguins tied the series again in the next game. That set up Game 7. There was one problem. The game was in Detroit. In the long history of the Stanley Cup Final, only two teams had ever won Game 7 on the road.

Early in the second period, Crosby chased the puck along the side wall. Detroit's Johan Franzén crushed him into the boards. Crosby hobbled off the ice. The young captain had led the team all year. In his absence, his teammates stepped up.

Maxime Talbot scored his second goal of the game a few minutes later. It put Pittsburgh up 2–0. Then goalie Marc-André Fleury made big save after

•EVGENI MALKIN

Center Evgeni Malkin was sometimes overshadowed by Crosby. The Russian was hardly a sidekick, though. That showed in the 2009 playoffs. Malkin recorded 36 points in 24 games. He was also awarded the Conn Smythe Trophy. That award is given to the best player of the playoffs.

Sidney Crosby hoists the Stanley Cup in Detroit.

big save. Pittsburgh held on and won the game 2–1. Crosby, at 21 years old, became the youngest captain to lift the Stanley Cup. And his career was only just beginning.

2

The Penguins
played in the
Civic Arena from
1967 to 2010.

PENGUINS TAKE FLIGHT

From 1942 to 1967, the NHL had only six teams. But in 1967, the league doubled in size. Pittsburgh was awarded one of the new teams. The city already had a place for the team to play. The round-topped Civic Arena was nicknamed "the Igloo." So when fans were asked to help pick a name for the team, they chose Penguins.

The Penguins didn't do much winning early on. That started to change when Michel Brière arrived. The young center was a breakout star as a rookie in 1969–70. Though just 5-foot-10 and 165 pounds, he made plays all over the ice. That helped Pittsburgh reach the playoffs for the first time. Sadly, Brière got in a car wreck that spring. He died a year later. After that, it took a few more years for Pittsburgh to find success.

In 1975, the Penguins finally reached the playoffs again. In fact, they made the playoffs in seven of the next eight seasons. But by the mid-1980s, Pittsburgh was back at the bottom of the standings. The low point came in 1983–84. That

Michel Brière (21) handles the puck in the 1970 playoffs.

season, the Penguins recorded the worst
record in team history. They won just 16 of
80 games.

All of that losing brought a reward,
though. The Penguins got the top pick

in the draft. They used it on a promising young center from Quebec. Mario Lemieux had just turned 19 when he joined the Penguins. In his rookie season, Lemieux tallied 100 points. By 1988–89, he had nearly doubled that, scoring 199. No one in the NHL had more goals or assists that season. Unfortunately for Penguins fans, the team still wasn't winning.

Pittsburgh added other skilled players in the late 1980s. They included defenseman Paul Coffey and goalie Tom

PITTSBURGH BLACK AND GOLD

The Penguins originally wore blue and white uniforms. In 1980, they switched to black and gold. Those colors match the city's flag. They're also the colors of Pittsburgh's other two major teams, the Steelers and the Pirates.

Mario Lemieux celebrates his first NHL goal.

Barrasso. However, entering the 1990–91 season, the Penguins had made just one playoff appearance in the previous eight seasons.

3

Jaromír Jágr scored 439 goals as a member of the Penguins.

MARIO'S WORLD

With the fifth pick in the 1990 draft, Pittsburgh selected Jaromír Jágr. The talented Czech winger helped put the Penguins over the top. For the first time, Pittsburgh won the division title. Then the team charged through the playoffs all the way to its first Stanley Cup Final.

The upstart Minnesota North Stars awaited. And Minnesota started the series with a 5–4 win in Pittsburgh. The Penguins soon roared back, though. Mario Lemieux stole the show in Game 2. Late in the second period, he collected the puck in his own zone. Then he raced up the ice, splitting two defenders. Finally, he deked the goalie and scored. The Penguins won the game 4–1. They went on to win the series. Pittsburgh clinched the Cup in Game 6 with an 8–0 win at Minnesota.

The Penguins were back in the Final the following season. In Game 1, they trailed the Chicago Blackhawks 4–1. However, Pittsburgh battled back and tied the game. Then, with only 13 seconds left in the third period, Lemieux buried a power play goal. It gave Pittsburgh a 5–4

Mario Lemieux celebrates a Stanley Cup victory with his teammates in 1992.

victory. The Penguins went on to sweep Chicago in four games.

For the second year in a row, Lemieux won the Conn Smythe Trophy. Jágr was well on his way to becoming a superstar, too. Other talented players, such as forward Martin Straka and defenseman

Sergei Zubov, arrived in the coming years. However, Lemieux began having health problems. In 1997, he retired.

Lemieux rejoined the Penguins in 2000. By then, much of the other talent was gone. The Penguins bottomed out in the early 2000s. But help was on the way. With the second pick in 2004, the team selected Evgeni Malkin. Then with the top pick in 2005, the Penguins chose Sidney Crosby.

A NEW OWNER

In the late 1990s, the Penguins were having financial trouble. They also still owed Mario Lemieux more than $30 million in salary. The former captain had an idea. Instead of being paid, he became the team's primary owner. As part of taking over, he promised to keep the team in Pittsburgh.

Martin Straka celebrates a goal against the Washington Capitals during the 1999–2000 season.

MARIO LEMIEUX

The Penguins were one of the NHL's worst teams in the early 1980s. Then Mario Lemieux arrived. A few years later, he led the team to back-to-back Stanley Cups. The hulking center went on to become one of hockey's all-time greats.

Lemieux stood 6-foot-4 and weighed 220 pounds. But he also had soft hands, and he was an elite skater. That combination made him a nightmare for defenders.

Few players could match his offensive production. "Super Mario" led the league in scoring six times. That is especially impressive because he played in the same era as Wayne Gretzky. Gretzky is the NHL's all-time leading scorer by a wide margin.

Mario Lemieux retired as the Penguins'
all-time leader in points (1,723), goals
(690), and assists (1,033).

Lemieux might have done even more.
However, serious health issues forced him out of
the game twice. He retired for good in 2006. But
Lemieux's legacy with the team continued as the
Penguins' owner.

4

Sidney Crosby battles for the puck in his rookie season.

SID TAKES OVER

Hockey fans first heard of Sidney Crosby when he was a youth player. Many predicted he could be a once-in-a-generation star. He quickly got to work proving them right.

As a rookie in 2005–06, Crosby scored 102 points. Most years, that would have been good enough to win the Calder Memorial Trophy as the NHL's top rookie.

But Crosby finished second. Washington Capitals winger Alex Ovechkin had scored 106 points. It was the first of many times the two stars would be compared.

Other than Crosby, Penguins fans didn't have much to cheer for that season. However, Evgeni Malkin arrived in 2006. Before long, the wins started piling up. Pittsburgh ended a four-year playoff drought in 2007. One year later, the team reached the Stanley Cup Final. And in 2009, the Penguins won it all.

•ROOMMATES

Mario Lemieux knew a thing or two about being a young NHL star. So when Sidney Crosby arrived in 2005, Lemieux invited the teenager to move in with him. Crosby lived with Lemieux until 2010. The experience helped Crosby learn how to be a successful pro athlete.

Evgeni Malkin jumps into the boards after scoring in the 2009 Stanley Cup Final.

Along the way, Pittsburgh beat Washington in the playoffs. In Game 2 of that series, Crosby and Ovechkin both scored hat tricks. Their rivalry helped create new interest in the league. But in 2011, Crosby suffered a concussion. From 2010–11 to 2012–13, he played in just 99 games.

By 2015–16, Crosby was back to his old form. Late in the season, veteran goalie Marc-André Fleury was injured. Matt Murray, a 21-year-old rookie, stepped up. His hot goaltending helped Pittsburgh make a run to another championship. This time, the Penguins defeated the San Jose Sharks.

One year later, another rookie shined. Center Jake Guentzel led the Penguins with 13 goals in the playoffs. They beat the Nashville Predators in the Final. That made Pittsburgh the first team to win back-to-back Cups since the Red Wings did it in 1997 and 1998. Crosby earned the Conn Smythe Trophy for both of Pittsburgh's Cup wins.

Matt Murray makes a save in the 2016 Stanley Cup Final.

Behind Crosby and Malkin, the Penguins remained competitive. In 2021, they made the playoffs for the 15th season in a row. Penguins fans hoped there would be plenty more to celebrate in the years to come.

• PITTSBURGH PENGUINS
QUICK STATS

FOUNDED: 1967

STANLEY CUP CHAMPIONSHIPS: 5 (1991, 1992, 2009, 2016, 2017)

KEY COACHES:

- Scotty Bowman (1991–93): 95 wins, 53 losses, 16 ties

- Dan Bylsma (2009–14): 252 wins, 117 losses, 32 overtime losses

- Mike Sullivan (2016–): 277 wins, 141 losses, 48 overtime losses

HOME ARENA: PPG Paints Arena (Pittsburgh, PA)

MOST CAREER POINTS: Mario Lemieux (1,723)

MOST CAREER GOALS: Mario Lemieux (690)

MOST CAREER ASSISTS: Mario Lemieux (1,033)

MOST CAREER SHUTOUTS: Marc-André Fleury (44)

Stats are accurate through the 2020–21 season.

GLOSSARY

ASSISTS
Passes, rebounds, or deflections that result in goals.

CONCUSSION
A brain injury that is usually caused by a blow to the head.

DEKE
To fake a movement in a certain direction to confuse an opponent.

DRAFT
An event that allows teams to choose new players coming into the league.

POINT
A statistic that a player earns by scoring a goal or having an assist.

RIVALRY
An ongoing competition that brings out the greatest emotion from fans and players.

ROOKIE
A professional athlete in his or her first year of competition.

VETERAN
A player who has spent several years in a league.

• TO LEARN
MORE

BOOKS

Duling, Kaitlyn. *Women in Hockey*. Lake Elmo, MN: Focus Readers, 2020.

Graves, Will. *Pro Hockey Upsets*. Minneapolis: Lerner Publications, 2020.

Hall, Brian. *Sidney Crosby: Hockey Star*. Lake Elmo, MN: Focus Readers, 2018.

MORE INFORMATION

To learn more about the Pittsburgh Penguins, go to **pressboxbooks.com/AllAccess**.

These links are routinely monitored and updated to provide the most current information available.

INDEX